Publishe
REARDON PUE
PO Box 919, Cheltenham,
www.reardon
email: reardon@bi

3rd Edition 2008

First Published © 1992
REARDON & SON

Written & illustrated
by
Mark Richards

ISBN 1 873877870
isbn (13) 9781873877876

Printed by
IN2PRINT
Cheltenham, England

William Wood's landscaped stream at Cornwell Manor (private).

CHIPPING NORTON

Walking is the healthiest and arguably the most satisfying of all outdoor freetime pursuits. The quest for seasonal beauty and new perspectives on familiar scenes form the genesis to develop a regular walking habit. For all who enjoy a good walk this selection of circular country excursions should provide the impetus to explore the quiet Cotswold countryside that embraces this fine old market town. The path network extending round the compass from Chipping Norton presents tremendous scope for rural rambles far from the madding car. Use this guide as a starting point, then buy the Ordnance Survey Pathfinder maps to find your own way. If of a gregarious disposition perhaps you may consider joining Chipping Norton Rambling Club, contact: Mrs Diana Rose, 55 Burford Road, tel. 642661. For a broader appreciation of walking opportunties in the west Oxfordshire countryside contact the local Ramblers' Association secretary: Mr Alan Cobb, Hillside Cottage, Dyers Hill, Charlbury, Chipping Norton OX7 3QD, tel. 0608 810283.

The Walks

pages		miles full	miles short	time hours	en route pub	en route shop
4 - 5	Swing Swang Walk	5		2½	✓	✓
6 - 9	Swailsford Valley Walk	6		3¼	✓	
10-11	Sarsbrook Valley Walk	6	3¾	3½	✓	
12-13	Hawk Stone Walk	7½	4	4	✓	✓
14-16	Glyme Valley Walk	11	8	4½	✓	✓

Each walk is depicted on a Highspy View which is an imaginary aerial perspective not subject to the graphic inhibitions of scaled mapping. Distance accomplished being shown in miles thus 5. The recommended route, whether footpath, bridleway, footway or minor road verge, is indicated by circles thus ○ ○ ○ ○, other paths are shown by dashes. Abbreviations employed are:
s = stile, K = kissing-gate, g = hand-gate, G = field-gate
fb = footbridge, ph = public house, TIC = Tourist Information Centre.

SWING SWANG WALK

5 miles allow 2½ hours

This is the natural close country circuit of Chipping Norton.

START from the Town Hall: Follow the footways of West Street and Burford Road. At the secondary school branch left along the Glyme Road (lane) passing Glyme Farm on the right via stiles and a footbridge. Beyond the strip lynchet terraces pass through a young plantation via stiles. Pass the ruined cottage to enter Cow Ditch Lane from the valley pasture.

Go left within this ancient lane, which becomes an unenclosed road passing New Chalford Farm. Cross London Road following the Swing Swang green lane to the A34, go left by Chapel House. Cross the Banbury Road at the roundabout beside the Shell Shop garage, entering Over Norton Park via the kissing gate. Follow the path strip downhill passing a remote cottage to a squeeze gap at the brook crossing; ascend the pasture to a second squeeze.

On entering Over Norton, go left along the footway round Cleeves Corner descend the hill, nearing the foot of the dip cross to a kissing gate. Follow the Cleeves Path passing an attractive pond before slipping through an underpass and rising along a fenced pasture top to the Castle Mound at the foot of Church Lane.

Either go directly into the churchyard or bear right down the pathway signposted to 'Pool Meadow'. At the bottom go left skirting round Pool Meadow (which can, indeed, be wet) keeping left to ascend the steps beside the Old Rectory gardens panel fence. Reaching a handgate turn left onto the path up through the churchyard. Ascend Church Street, crossing Spring Street continue into Middle Row and the Market Place. □

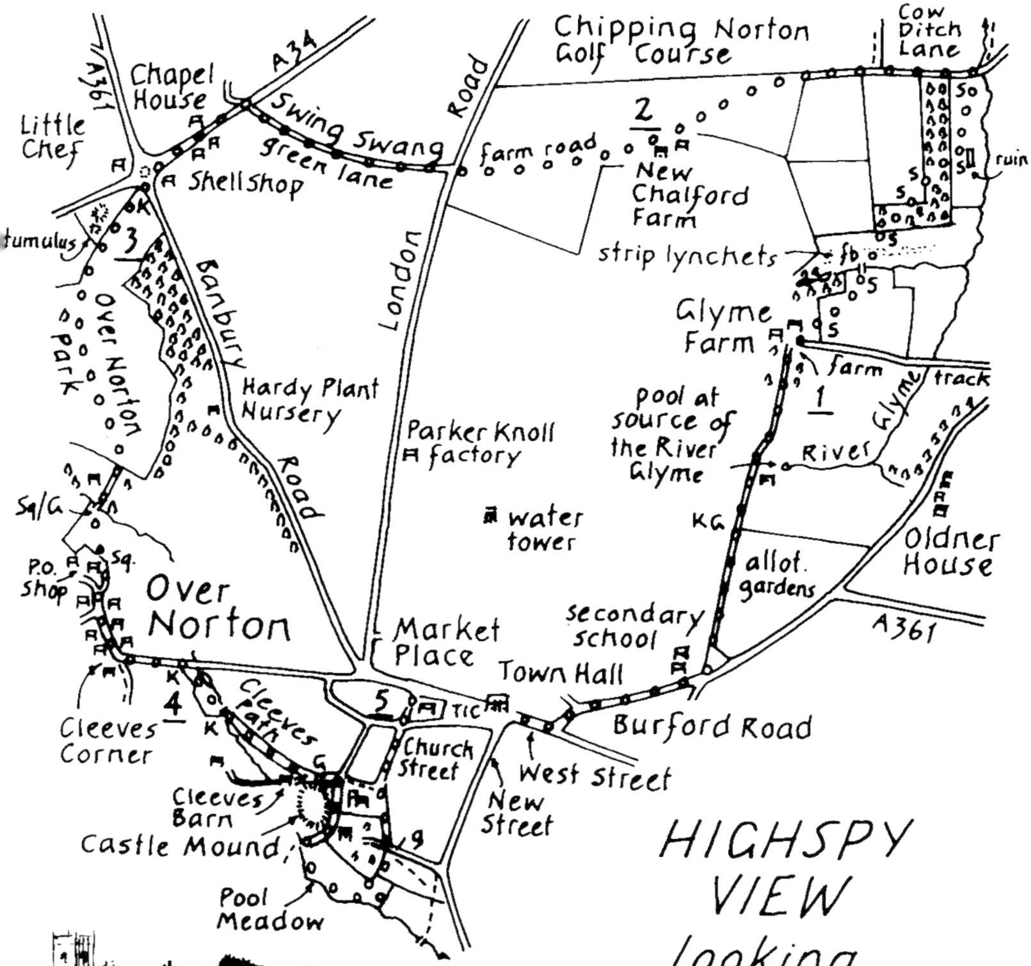
Chipping Norton Golf Course
Cow Ditch Lane
A34
A361
Chapel House
Little Chef
Swing Swang green lane
London Road
farm road
2
New Chalford Farm
ruin
Shell shop
tumulus
3
Banbury Road
Over Norton Park
strip lynchets
fb
Glyme Farm
farm track
Glyme
1
Hardy Plant Nursery
pool at source of the River Glyme
River
Parker Knoll factory
Sq/G
KG
water tower
Oldner House
allot. gardens
P.O. Shop
Sq.
Over Norton
secondary school
A361
Market Place
Town Hall
4
5
TIC
Cleeves Corner
Cleeves Path
Burford Road
Church Street
West Street
New Street
Cleeves Barn
Castle Mound
Pool Meadow

HIGHSPY VIEW looking EAST

St. Mary's parish church and the Castle Mound from Cleeves Path

SWAILSFORD VALLEY WALK

6 miles allow 3¼ hours

A thoroughly relaxing walk in pastoral scenery, reaching out across the Swailsford Brook valley to visit Cornwell and Salford.

START from the Town Hall: Follow New Street down to a kissing gate on the left opposite Penhurst NCH School. Cross the pasture diagonally descend to a stile at the foot of the dell.

Follow the roadway left, then go right within the security fenced path, cross the access lane to Bliss Mill. From the facing stile ascend The Common half left to the kissing gate onto the footway. Keep left, beside the A44, approaching Southerndown the footway is lost, immediately after the nursing home go left along the access road. The tarmac road bears left to Hill Farm but continue within the bridle lane. Proceed along the uncultivated strip across the arable field to reach a stile and footbridge over Swailsford Brook.

Cross the ensuing meadow, latterly beside the fence to the gate onto a minor road, cross straight over. Follow the hedge, when this bends left pass through the gap to descend the arable field on a clear bridle path to a gate. Follow the road, keeping left at the fork, short-cut the next bend, pass the wrought-iron gates with the delighful vista of Cornwell Manor and gardens. Advance to the road junction, by the telephone kiosk go right.

Ascending past the stable-yard. Bear right at the top of the estate village, follow the church path, via an orchard and metal fenced pathway to pass through St. Peter's churchyard. From the kissing gate, beneath a yew, descend the pasture, passing through the valley passage rise to a kissing gate onto the byway. Go right, then left along the drive to Glebe Farm, keep right ▷

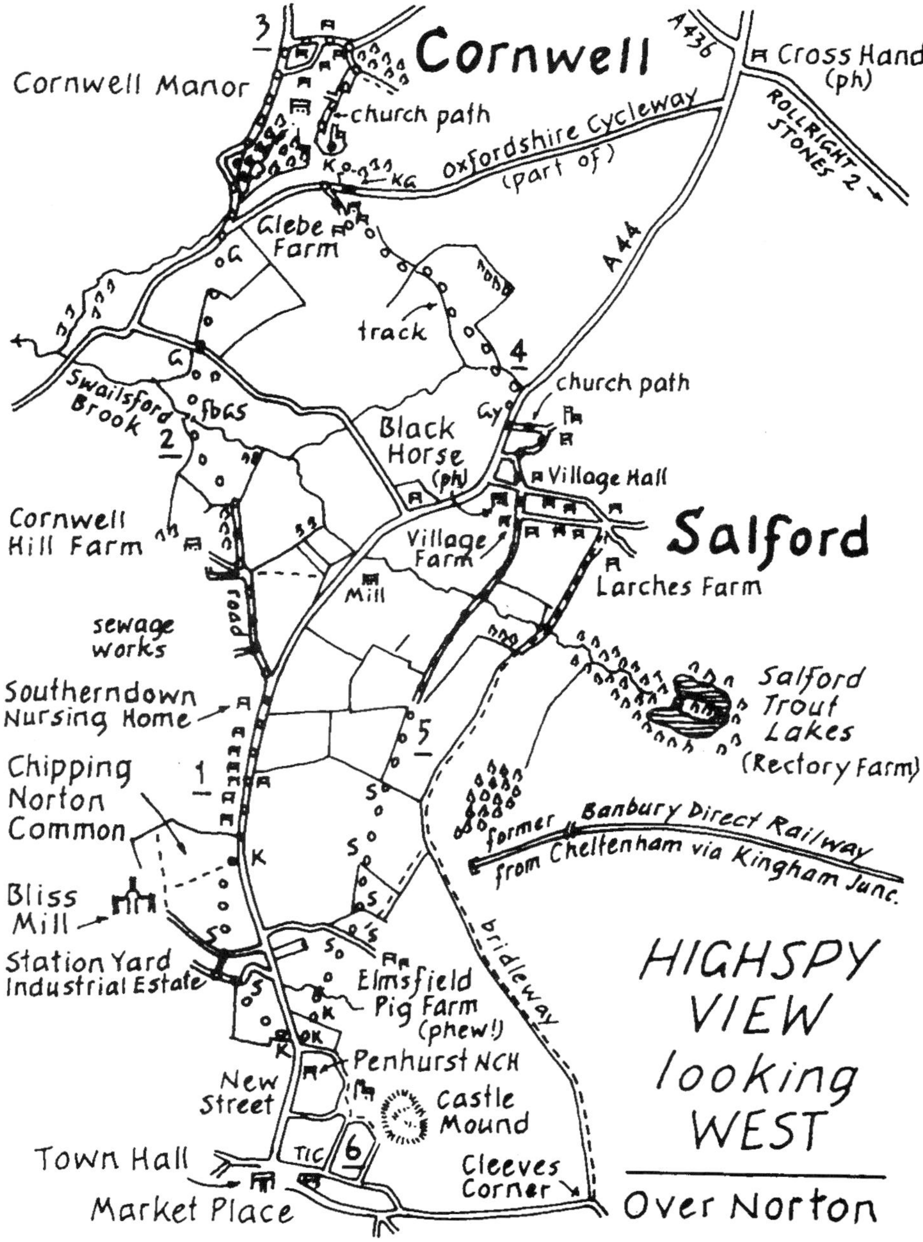

Cornwell
Cornwell Manor
church path
Oxfordshire Cycleway
(part of)
A436
Cross Hands
(ph)
ROLLRIGHT STONES 2
Glebe Farm
track
A44
Swailsford Brook
church path
Black Horse
(ph)
Village Hall
Salford
Cornwell Hill Farm
Village Farm
Mill
Larches Farm
road
sewage works
Southerndown Nursing Home
Salford Trout Lakes
(Rectory Farm)
Chipping Norton Common
former Banbury Direct Railway
from Cheltenham via Kingham Junc.
Bliss Mill
Station Yard Industrial Estate
bridleway
Elmsfield Pig Farm
(phew!)
Penhurst NCH
New Street
Castle Mound
TIC
Town Hall
Market Place
Cleeves Corner
HIGHSPY VIEW looking WEST
Over Norton

The south front of Cornwell Manor as seen through the vista gate

▷ between the grain barns, then continue along the field access track (bridleway) to a gateway on the A44. Cross the busy road, with the utmost care, follow the verge to the fenced footpath leading to St. Mary's church.

Go right, down the road passing the village hall, following the Lower End road pass through Village Farm. Continue up the dairy pasture access gangway, at the end keep the ascending hedge to the right in ascending to the stile. A clear path up the ensuing arable field leads to a sequence of stiles in descending into the valley below Elmsfield Farm, rise into the recreation field via kissing gates regain New Street. □

Bliss Mill from Chipping Norton Common.

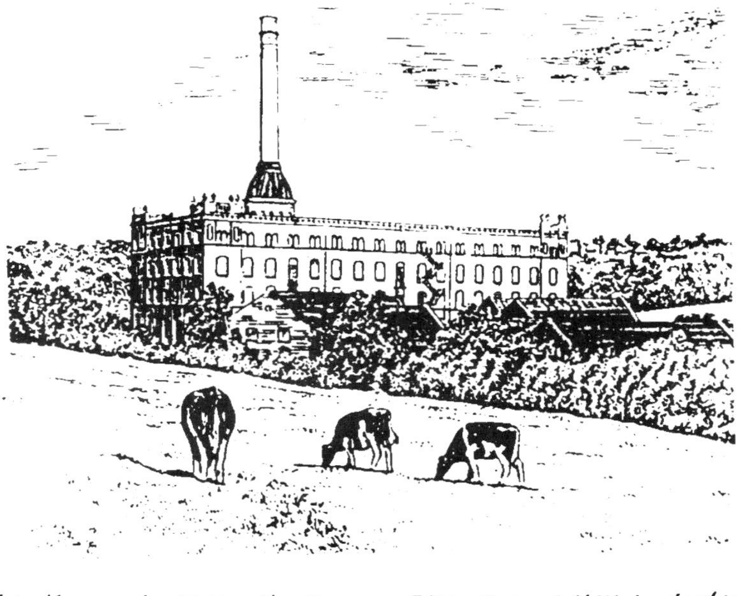

Closed in the early 1970s, the former Bliss Tweed Mill is destined to become a luxurious twenty-first century apartment block.

SARSBROOK VALLEY WALK

6 miles allow 3½ hours

A delightful excursion south west into the Sarsbrook combe visiting Sarsden and Churchill. Best entertained as a short walk from Old London Road, giving a walk of just 3½ miles.

START from the Town Hall: Follow either Churchill and Hailey or Burford and Walterbush Roads to reach the Town football ground. Follow the open ended road beside the ground to a footpath sign directing half right across arable land. At the junction of hedges the footpath bears half left ascending the large arable field to a gateway onto Old London Road: an instance where if the corn is high the walker will find it less taxing to follow the hedge left keeping to the headland.

START from Old London Road: Go right, then left, along the access road to Sarsgrove Farm. Where this bears left, go right along the gallop, then left, down beside the wall to a gateway just below a trough. Continue down the field to cross the lower gallop to a gateway. Descend the arable field down the ridge and subsequent bank to a bridge over Sars Brook and gate.

Ascend the pasture bank, keeping above the spring, pass close by the house at Parsonage Farm. Contour below the wall to a fence gate, shortly after bear half right to the gate below a stone hovel. Follow the fence and 'ha-ha' before dipping through a stream hollow to rise to a gate, go right. Descending pass to the left of a stone barn to cross Sars Brook again. Ascend the deeply corrugated ridge and furrow pasture half left to a fence in the corner. Follow the bank top path ascending beside the road pass All Saint's bearing right to cross the recreation field. Follow the footway along Chipping Norton Road before branching right up Besbury Lane to reunite with the outward journey at the Sarsgrove access road. □

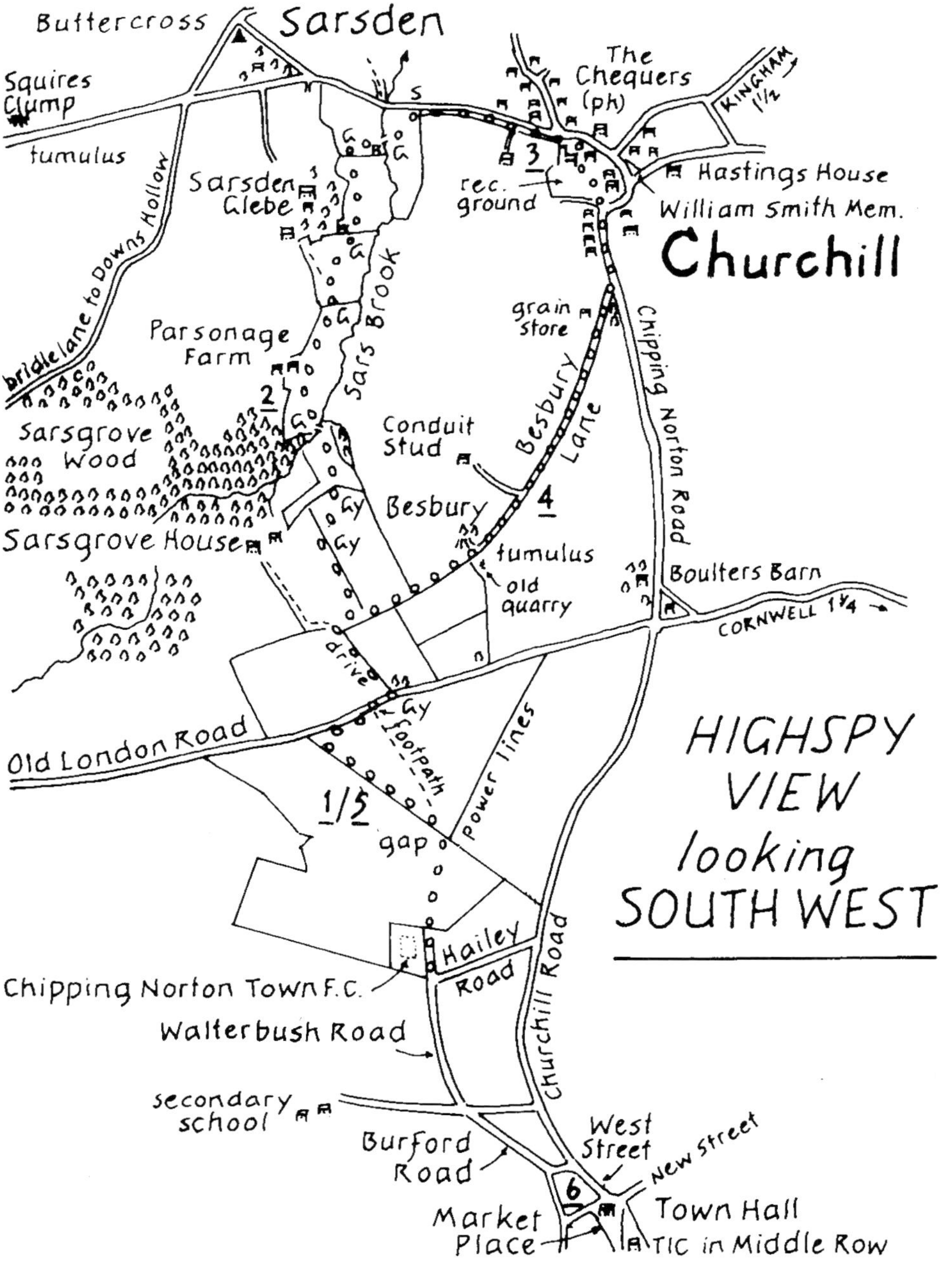

Buttercross
Sarsden
Squires Clump
tumulus
Sarsden Glebe
The Chequers (ph)
KINGHAM 1½
Hastings House
William Smith Mem.
rec. ground
Churchill
bridlelane to Downs Hollow
Parsonage Farm
Sars Brook
grain store
Chipping Norton Road
Besbury Lane
Conduit Stud
Sarsgrove Wood
Besbury
Sarsgrove House
tumulus
old quarry
Boulters Barn
CORNWELL 1¼
drive
Old London Road
footpath
power lines
HIGHSPY VIEW looking SOUTH WEST
gap
Hailey Road
Churchill Road
Chipping Norton Town F.C.
Walterbush Road
secondary school
Burford Road
West Street
New Street
Market Place
Town Hall
TIC in Middle Row

HAWK STONE WALK

$7\frac{1}{2}$ miles allow 4 hours

A fine walk featuring a mystic megalith and a lovely lane. Begun from East Downs the walk can be shortened to $4\frac{1}{4}$ miles.

START *from Town Hall*: Follow West Street and Burford Road beyond The Albion take the Charlbury Road at the junction. Within 30 yards a footpath sign 'Dean 3' directs right. This is the beginning of an unbroken sequence of thirteen arable fields, at (most) moments of doubt a reassuring waymark is at hand, so there is no need to fear embarking on this adventure. Tractor wheelmark reinstatement provides on the ground guidance on the traverse of the old airfield to Old London Road.

START *from the verge near East Downs Farm*: Follow the road to the footpath sign beyond the entrance to Galleypot Farm and opposite the stile off the airfield approach. Continue with the path undaunted by seasonal cropping, trend half left, before angling right to pass Claridge's Barn via a series of gaps all the way down to the Hawk Stone. This weathered orthostat the old haunt of hawks, is the last surviving stone from a bronze age burial mound, probably contemporary with The Whispering Knights.

Continue to join the quiet byway leading down to Dean Manor. At the lefthand bend go through the gate, follow the bridleway right, descend to a bridle gate at the crossing of Little Dean Brook. Rise into a short lane, thereby joining the street into Chadlington. Advance past St. Nicholas' church and turn right up Church Road, at the left bend, beside the Bowls Club enter Green Lane. Reaching Old London Road go left, passing Limekiln Cottage, taking an unsignposted right turn through the gate onto a track leading to Chadlington Downs Farm. Pass left between the barns to traverse a last arable field to reach the footway at Bellpiece, follow the A361 back into town. □

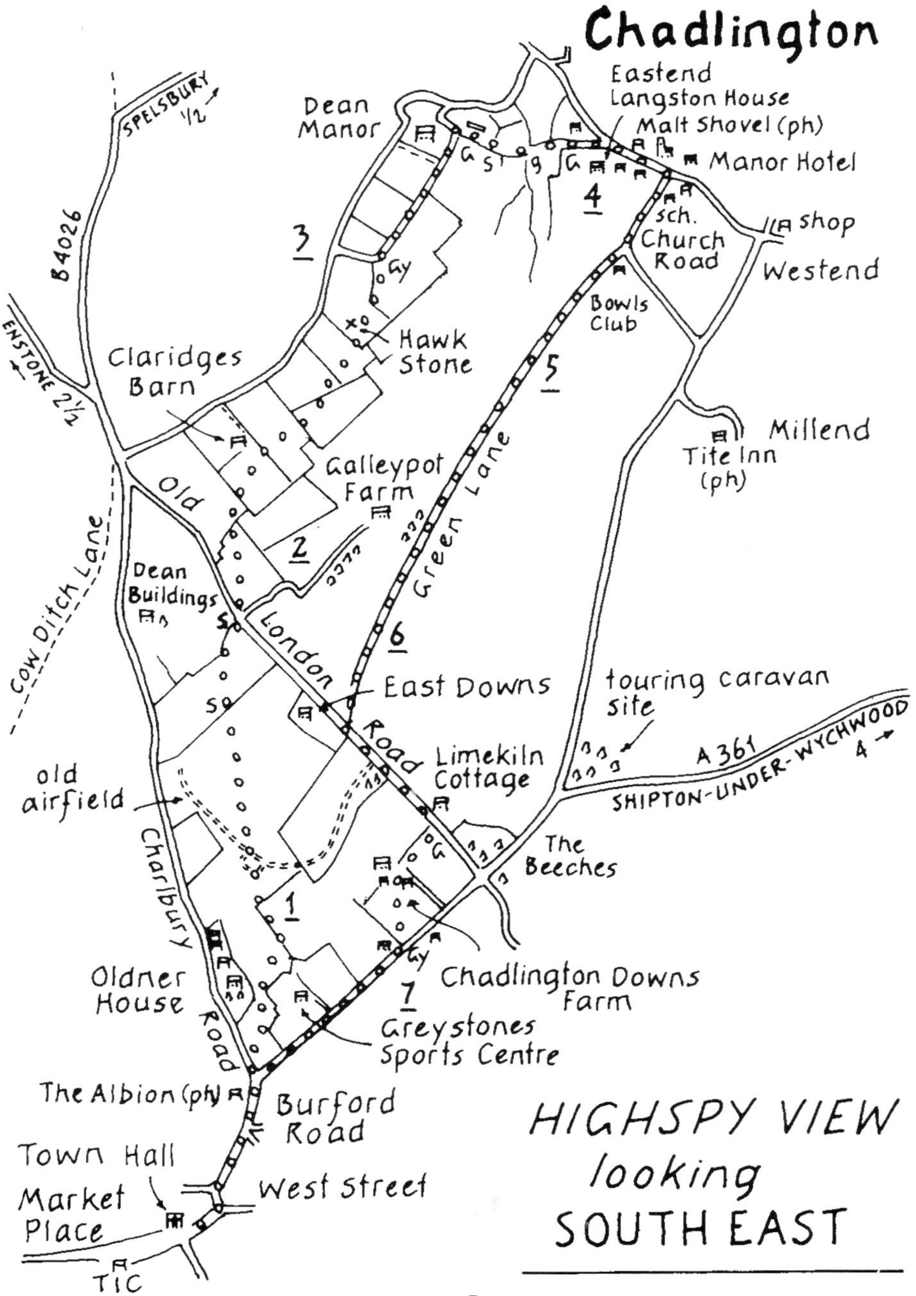
Chadlington
Eastend
Langston House
Malt Shovel (ph)
Manor Hotel
Dean Manor
SPELSBURY 1/2
B4026
ENSTONE 2 1/2
shop
Westend
sch.
Church Road
Bowls Club
Hawk Stone
Claridges Barn
Millend
Tite Inn (ph)
Galleypot Farm
Green Lane
Old
London Road
Cow Ditch Lane
Dean Buildings
East Downs
touring caravan site
A 361
SHIPTON-UNDER-WYCHWOOD 4
Limekiln Cottage
old airfield
The Beeches
Charlbury Road
Chadlington Downs Farm
Oldner House
Greystones Sports Centre
The Albion (ph)
Burford Road
Town Hall
Market Place
West Street
TIC
1
2
3
4
5
6
7

HIGHSPY VIEW looking SOUTH EAST

GLYME VALLEY WALK

8 miles allow 4½ hours

A satisfying stroll down the Glyme to Church Enstone via the medieval lost village of Nether Chalford and through Lidstone, returning via Heythrop Park and Cow Ditch Lane.

START from Town Hall: consult the Swing Swang Walk.

START from Chalford Green, situated 2 miles out of town on the B4026 opposite the Dean turn: Follow Cow Ditch Lane for 300 yards to where it narrows, branch right through the bridle gate (galvanised). The farm trackway leads towards Old Chalford Farm, at the bend, short of the farmhouse, go right via the stile.

Traverse the pasture with the tractor tracks to a gate then follow the fence, pass the site of Nether Chalford. Then, via a second galvanised bridle gate, continue through Stone Farm, and along the drive to the road. Go left down the Lidstone street. At the foot of the hill cross the stile right (respect private nature reserve). Follow the winding path via a stile, up and along the headland glance past the top of woodland before traversing an arable field to the A34. Proceed via facing stone stiles, bear half right, crossing Manor Farm drive to the hedge gap.

Traverse the arable field to the bridleway strip, crossing this pass through the wall gap, cross the ensuing arable field to a stile (with large-scale footpath map affixed). Go through the paddock via a stile to cross the Heythrop Park drive. Descend the bank passing in front of the old mill, ascend Mill Lane advancing beyond The Crown to the lych-gate of St. Kenelm's.

Follow the 'Heythrop' footpath left. At the end of the confined path pass via a tall handgate, through the shaded enclosure, to a stile. Cross the track via a stile then go left around the edge ▷

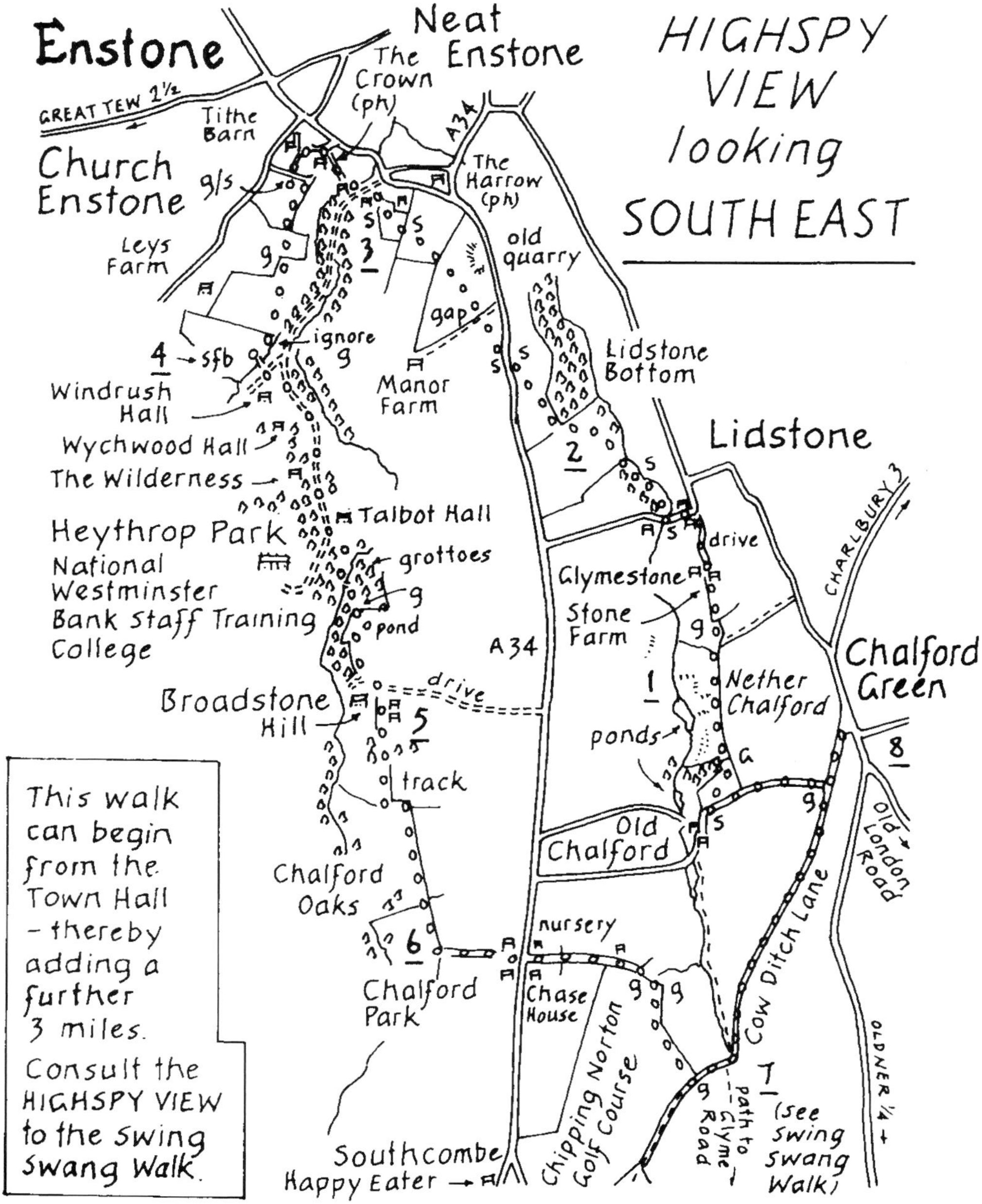
HIGHSPY VIEW looking SOUTH EAST
Enstone
Neat Enstone
The Crown (ph)
GREAT TEW 1½
Tithe Barn
Church Enstone
g/s
A34
The Harrow (ph)
old quarry
Leys Farm
3
gap
ignore g
4 → sfb
Manor Farm
Lidstone Bottom
Windrush Hall
Wychwood Hall
The Wilderness
Lidstone
2
Talbot Hall
Heythrop Park
National Westminster Bank Staff Training College
grottoes
pond
drive
Glymestone
Stone Farm
CHARLBURY 3
A34
Chalford Green
1
Nether Chalford
Broadstone Hill
5
ponds
8
track
Old Chalford
Old London Road
Chalford Oaks
Cow Ditch Lane
nursery
6
Chalford Park
Chase House
Chipping Norton Golf Course
OLDNER ¼
7 (see Swing Swang Walk)
path to Glyme Road
Southcombe
Happy Eater
This walk can begin from the Town Hall – thereby adding a further 3 miles.
Consult the HIGHSPY VIEW to the Swing Swang Walk.

▷ of the arable field. At the second righthand turn maintain course across the arable field to the bridle gate. Follow the headland for 120 yards then bear half left, down the arable field, to an old handgate. Ignoring the inviting handgate in the dip continue across the rough bank to the stile and footbridge.

Joining the footway beside the Heythrop Park main drive advance to Talbot Hall, branch half left down the trackway passing two grottoes. Guided by waymarking cross the stream rising to a bridle gate. Reaching the pond go right, beside the fenced horse paddock, to the open road before Broadstone Hill House. Keep left then right to join the track running below the huge de-luxe barns. Stay on this bridle track all the way to Chalford Park. Cross the busy A34 following the lane downhill via bridle gates, slipping through a side valley before rising within the golf course to re-enter Cow Ditch Lane. Either go left crossing the infant Glyme to reach Chalford Green, or go right to Oxford Road for a direct return to the Market Place along footways. □

Lidstone

cont

British & North American Readers:
Please note that Australian cup and spoon measurements are metric. A quic conversion guide appears on page 6 A glossary explaining unfamiliar terms and ingredients begins on page 60.

2 getting ready to party

Preparation is the key to your party running like clockwork. And with a little forethought, you'll be happily mingling with guests rather than being chained to the kitchen.

Do ahead

Wherever possible, the best way to free yourself to have fun on the night is to do what you can ahead of time. Make a series of lists that will help you achieve this end. For example, divide your shopping list into those items that are non-perishable and those that are perishable; purchase the non-perishables well ahead so that, come the day of the party, your shopping list is drastically reduced. Next, plan your cooking timetable – try to choose recipes that are suitable for freezing; thawing and reheating will always save precious time. Something else to consider: do you have enough plates, cutlery, tables, chairs, glasses, linen, trays, and so forth, to service your needs? If not, ask friends and relatives for their help, or it may be simpler to hire the things you need. Before committing to one hire company, shop around; prices can vary markedly. If your budget extends to it, you can also hire someone to serve the food and clean up – many agencies provide these services for a relatively inexpensive fee.

How much is enough?

One of the most vexing problems you will encounter in planning your party is trying to estimate just how much food and drink you will need. Each recipe in this book states how many savouries it makes; this should help in your preparation. As a general guide, allow six pieces per person for the first hour, and another four pieces per person for every subsequent hour. When planning your menu, give some thought to the occasion and the time of year. Aim for a mix of hot and cold savouries, but tend toward a greater proportion of hot in winter and cold in summer. If desired, you can indicate the close of the party by serving some delicious chocolates or petits fours with coffee.

Drink up
Drinks are even more difficult to estimate than food. You may wish to serve cocktails when the guests arrive, or simply beer and sparkling, white and red wines. Non-alcoholic drinks are essential; juices, mineral water and soft drinks should be readily available for the consumption of "designated drivers" or those who don't drink alcohol. It's helpful to put drinks in a readily accessible spot so that guests can help themselves without getting in the way of any frantic activity in the kitchen! Of course, don't forget the ice, plenty of napkins and, if serving cocktails, drinking straws.

4 spanakopita

1.5kg silverbeet, trimmed

1 tablespoon olive oil

1 medium brown onion (150g), chopped finely

2 cloves garlic, crushed

1 teaspoon ground nutmeg

200g fetta, crumbled

1 tablespoon finely grated lemon rind

1/4 cup coarsely chopped fresh mint

1/4 cup coarsely chopped fresh flat-leaf parsley

1/4 cup coarsely chopped fresh dill

4 green onions, chopped finely

16 sheets fillo pastry

125g butter, melted

2 teaspoons sesame seeds

Boil, steam or microwave silverbeet until just wilted; drain. Squeeze out excess moisture; drain on absorbent paper. Chop silverbeet coarsely; spread out on absorbent paper.

Heat oil in small frying pan; cook brown onion and garlic, stirring, until onion is soft. Add nutmeg; cook, stirring, until fragrant. Combine onion mixture and silverbeet in large bowl with fetta, rind, herbs and green onion.

Brush one sheet of the fillo with butter; fold lengthways into thirds, brushing with butter between each fold.

Place a rounded tablespoon of the silverbeet mixture at bottom of one narrow edge of folded fillo sheet, leaving a border. Fold opposite corner of fillo diagonally across the filling to form large triangle; continue folding to end of fillo sheet, retaining triangular shape. Place on lightly oiled oven trays, seam-side down; repeat with remaining ingredients until 16 spanakopita are made.

Brush spanakopita with remaining butter; sprinkle with sesame seeds. Bake, uncovered, in moderate oven about 15 minutes or until browned lightly.

MAKES 16

Per serving 11.6g fat; 665kJ

6 little **caesar** salads

24 slices white sandwich bread

125g garlic butter, softened

3 bacon rashers (200g), chopped finely

1 baby cos lettuce, shredded finely

½ cup (125ml) caesar salad dressing

12 whole anchovy fillets, drained, halved lengthways

⅓ cup (25g) parmesan cheese flakes

Cut 8cm rounds from bread. Using a rolling pin, flatten bread rounds slightly. Spread both sides of the rounds with garlic butter. Press rounds into 24 unoiled patty pans. Bake, uncovered, in moderately hot oven about 15 minutes or until browned lightly and crisp; cool.
Cook bacon in small frying pan, stirring, until crisp; drain on absorbent paper.
Just before serving, combine the lettuce, bacon and dressing in medium bowl. Spoon the lettuce mixture into the bread cases; top each case with a rolled strip of anchovy and a parmesan flake.

MAKES 24
Per serving 8.5g fat; 596kJ

spicy **hoisin** chicken balls 7

1kg minced chicken

3 cups (210g) stale breadcrumbs

1 small brown onion (80g), chopped finely

2 cloves garlic, crushed

1 egg, beaten lightly

1/4 cup (60ml) hoisin sauce

1 tablespoon light soy sauce

2 teaspoons grated fresh ginger

1/2 teaspoon sesame oil

1/4 teaspoon five-spice powder

1/3 cup (80ml) peanut oil

dipping sauce

1/2 cup (125ml) sweet chilli sauce

2 tablespoons white wine vinegar

2 tablespoons finely chopped fresh coriander

Preheat oven to moderate. Combine chicken, breadcrumbs, onion, garlic, egg, sauces, ginger, sesame oil and five-spice in medium bowl; mix well. Shape level tablespoons of mixture into balls.
Heat peanut oil in large frying pan; cook chicken balls, in batches (shaking the pan to keep the round shape), until browned all over; drain on absorbent paper. Transfer chicken balls to oven tray; bake, uncovered, in moderate oven about 15 minutes or until cooked through.
Thread chicken balls onto skewers with lime and coriander, if desired; serve with dipping sauce.
Dipping Sauce Combine ingredients in small bowl.

MAKES 60
Per serving 2.9g fat; 232kJ

8 empanadas

400g can tomatoes

1 tablespoon olive oil

1 medium brown onion (150g), chopped finely

1 clove garlic, crushed

1 teaspoon cracked black pepper

1/2 teaspoon ground cinnamon

1/2 teaspoon ground clove

600g minced beef

1/4 cup (40g) raisins, chopped coarsely

1 tablespoon cider vinegar

1/4 cup (35g) slivered almonds, toasted

2 x 800g packages ready-rolled quiche pastry

1 egg, beaten lightly

vegetable oil, for deep-frying

Blend or process undrained tomatoes until smooth; reserve.

Heat oil in large heavy-base saucepan; cook onion, garlic and spices, stirring, until onion is soft. Add beef; cook, stirring, until changed in colour. Drain away excess fat from pan. Stir in tomato, raisins and vinegar; simmer, uncovered, about 20 minutes or until filling mixture thickens. Stir in nuts.

Cut 9cm rounds from pastry sheets (you need 32 rounds). Place a level tablespoon of beef mixture in centre of each round; brush edge lightly with egg. Fold pastry over to enclose filling, press edges together to seal.

Heat oil in large saucepan; deep-fry empanadas, in batches, until crisp and browned lightly, drain on absorbent paper. Serve immediately with a dollop of sour cream or bottled salsa, if desired.

MAKES 32

Per serving 6.5g fat; 416kJ

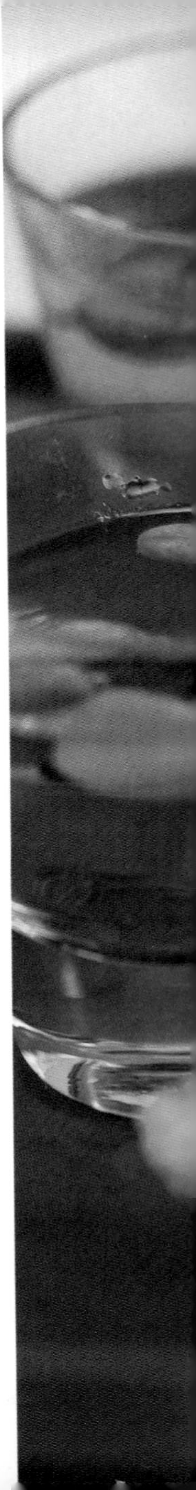

10 potatoes with sour cream and smoked salmon

24 tiny new potatoes (1kg)

200g packaged light spreadable cream cheese

2 tablespoons finely chopped fresh dill

100g smoked salmon slices

Preheat oven to moderately hot. Place potatoes in large oiled baking dish; bake, uncovered, in moderately hot oven about 45 minutes or until tender. Allow potatoes to cool for 15 minutes.

Meanwhile, combine cream cheese and dill in small bowl. Cut salmon slices into thin strips.

Cut a cross halfway through potatoes with a small knife, gently squeeze the base of the potatoes to open the centre.

Fill centres with a spoonful of cheese mixture, top with a salmon twist; top with extra dill, if desired.

MAKES 24

Per serving 1.6g fat; 204kJ

oven-baked vegetable crisps

cooking-oil spray

4 medium parsnips (500g)

4 medium potatoes (800g)

1 medium kumara (400g)

sea salt

Preheat oven to moderately slow. Spray two or three oven trays with cooking-oil spray. Cut parsnips into 2mm-thick slices using a mandoline, v-slicer or sharp knife.

Place parsnip slices in single layer on prepared oven trays, spray with a little more cooking-oil spray. Bake, uncovered, in moderately slow oven about 40 minutes or until crisp, turning halfway through cooking and removing smaller slices from trays when they are ready. Transfer to a wire rack to cool. Repeat with remaining vegetables.

Serve vegetable crisps sprinkled with a little salt.

SERVES 4

Per serving 1.3g fat; 1073kJ

12 dip platter

beetroot dip

2 large fresh beetroot (400g)

1 tablespoon tahini

2 teaspoons lemon juice

1/2 cup (140g) greek-style yogurt

Boil, steam or microwave beetroot until tender. Cool slightly; peel and chop coarsely. **Blend** or process beetroot with remaining ingredients until smooth.

MAKES 1 1/2 CUPS
Per tablespoon
1.2g fat; 103kJ

hummus

300g can chickpeas, rinsed, drained

1 clove garlic, quartered

1/4 teaspoon sweet paprika

1/4 cup (60ml) tahini

1/4 cup (60ml) lemon juice

2 tablespoons olive oil

2 tablespoons water

Blend or process ingredients until smooth.

MAKES 1 1/2 CUPS
Per tablespoon
2.3g fat; 124kJ

Front to back: spiced carrot dip; beetroot dip; hummus.

spiced carrot dip

2 large carrots (360g), chopped coarsely

1 tablespoon olive oil

1 clove garlic, crushed

1/2 teaspoon ground cumin

1/2 teaspoon ground coriander

1/4 teaspoon ground turmeric

1/2 cup (140g) greek-style yogurt

2 tablespoons finely chopped fresh coriander

Boil, steam or microwave carrot until soft; drain. **Heat** oil in medium frying pan; cook garlic and spices, stirring, until fragrant. Blend or process carrot and spice mixture with yogurt and coriander until smooth.

MAKES 1 1/2 CUPS
Per tablespoon
0.6g fat; 61kJ

14 roast **beef** croutes

1 small french bread stick

¼ cup (75g) whole-egg mayonnaise

360g thinly sliced rare roast beef

24 small fresh basil leaves

1 tablespoon horseradish cream

1 tablespoon chilli jam

Preheat oven to moderately hot. Remove and discard ends from breadstick; cut bread into 24 thin slices. Place bread slices, in single layer, on oven tray. Bake, uncovered, in moderately hot oven 15 minutes, turning halfway through baking, until browned on both sides; cool.
Just before serving, spread one side of the croutes with mayonnaise. Divide the beef among the croutes; top with basil leaves, then half with horseradish cream and the remaining half with chilli jam.

MAKES 24
Per serving 2g fat; 219kJ

mini pappadums with curried egg

3 hard-boiled eggs, shelled

1 tablespoon mayonnaise

1 tablespoon mango chutney

1 teaspoon mild curry paste

1 green onion, chopped finely

2 teaspoons finely chopped fresh coriander

75g packet ready-to-eat mini pappadums

Mash the eggs in a small bowl with mayonnaise, chutney and curry paste until combined. Stir in onion and coriander. **Just** before serving, top pappadums with teaspoonfuls of egg mixture. Top with chilli and green onion, if desired.

MAKES 20

Per serving

1.3g fat; 120kJ

16 oysters

oysters rockefeller

80g butter

2 cloves garlic, crushed

500g spinach, trimmed, chopped coarsely

24 medium oysters on the half shell (1.5kg)

1/3 cup (25g) stale breadcrumbs

Melt half of the butter in medium saucepan. Add garlic and spinach; cook, stirring, about 3 minutes or until spinach is wilted. **Place** oysters on oven tray; top with spinach mixture, sprinkle with breadcrumbs, drizzle with remaining melted butter. Grill until breadcrumbs are golden brown.

MAKES 24

Per serving

3.5g fat; 217kJ

oysters mornay

60g butter

1/3 cup (50g) plain flour

2 cups (500ml) milk

1/2 cup (60g) coarsely grated cheddar cheese

24 medium oysters on the half shell (1.5kg)

Melt butter in medium saucepan, add flour; cook, stirring, about 3 minutes or until mixture thickens and bubbles. **Remove** from heat, gradually stir in milk; cook, stirring, until mixture boils and thickens. Remove from heat, stir in half of the cheese. **Place** oysters on oven tray; spoon sauce onto oysters, sprinkle with remaining cheese. Grill until browned lightly.

MAKES 24

Per serving

4.3g fat; 294kJ

oysters kilpatrick

24 medium oysters on the half shell (1.5kg)

4 bacon rashers (280g), chopped finely

2 tablespoons worcestershire sauce

Place oysters on oven tray; top with bacon, drizzle with sauce.
Grill until bacon is crisp.

MAKES 24
Per serving
2.3g fat; 216kJ

left to right: oysters kilpatrick; oysters rockefeller; oysters mornay

18 mushroom palmiers

375g packet frozen puff pastry, thawed

1 egg, beaten lightly

filling

1 tablespoon vegetable oil

15g butter

2 cloves garlic, crushed

1 medium brown onion (150g), chopped finely

250g button mushrooms, chopped finely

1 tablespoon plain flour

2 tablespoons water

2 tablespoons finely chopped fresh chives

Roll pastry on floured surface to form 25cm x 35cm rectangle; cut in half lengthways to form two rectangles. Spread half of the filling over each rectangle. Fold long sides of each rectangle so they meet in the centre, brush along centre with some of the egg; fold in half, press lightly. Cover; refrigerate 30 minutes. Cut rolls into 1cm slices, place cut-side up on lightly oiled oven trays. Bake, uncovered, in moderately hot oven about 12 minutes or until browned.

Filling Heat oil and butter in medium frying pan; cook garlic and onion, stirring, until onion is soft. Stir in mushrooms; cook, stirring, about 5 minutes or until mushrooms are soft. Add flour; cook, stirring, 1 minute. Gradually stir in the water; cook, stirring, until mixture boils and thickens. Remove from heat; cool. Stir in chives.

MAKES 30

Per serving 4g fat; 260kJ

warm **corn** and chive dip

250g jar corn relish

1¼ cups (300g) sour cream

few drops Tabasco sauce

2 tablespoons finely chopped fresh chives

½ cup (60g) finely grated cheddar cheese

Combine ingredients in medium saucepan; stir over low heat until just warm.
Serve with corn chips, if desired.

MAKES 2 CUPS
Per tablespoon 5.9g fat; 293kJ

20 mussels with roasted garlic mayonnaise

1 small red capsicum (150g)

30 small black mussels (750g)

1 small brown onion (80g), chopped finely

1 cup (250ml) dry white wine

1 bay leaf

1 large silverbeet leaf (100g), shredded finely

roasted garlic mayonnaise

1 medium bulb garlic (90g)

1 tablespoon light olive oil

1 egg yolk

1 teaspoon dijon mustard

1 tablespoon lemon juice

2/3 cup (160ml) light olive oil, extra

pinch cayenne pepper

1 teaspoon freshly ground black pepper

1 teaspoon finely chopped fresh thyme

Quarter capsicum, remove and discard seeds and membranes. Roast under grill or in very hot oven, skin-side up, until skin blisters and blackens. Cover capsicum pieces with plastic or paper for 5 minutes, peel away skin, then cut capsicum into thin strips.

Scrub mussels, remove and discard beards. Combine onion, wine, bay leaf and mussels in large saucepan; cook, covered, over high heat, about 5 minutes or until mussels open (discard any unopened mussels). Remove and discard half of each mussel shell, remove mussels from remaining shells.

Place mussel shells on oven trays; divide silverbeet and capsicum among them, top each with one mussel and some roasted garlic mayonnaise. Just before serving, grill mussels until browned lightly.

Roasted Garlic Mayonnaise Preheat oven to moderately hot. Place whole garlic bulb on oven tray; drizzle with oil. Bake, uncovered, in moderately hot oven about 45 minutes or until very soft. Stand garlic 15 minutes; cut in half horizontally, squeeze out garlic pulp. Blend or process garlic pulp, egg yolk, mustard and juice until smooth. With motor operating, add extra oil in a thin stream. Stir in peppers and thyme.

MAKES 30

Per serving 5.8g fat; 251kJ

22 taramasalata

4 slices stale white sandwich bread

100g can tarama

1 small brown onion (80g), chopped coarsely

1 clove garlic, quartered

¼ cup (60ml) lemon juice

1½ cups (375ml) olive oil

Discard crusts from bread; soak bread in cold water for 2 minutes. Drain; squeeze water from bread using hands. **Blend** or process bread, tarama, onion, garlic and juice until combined. With motor operating, add oil in thin stream; process until mixture thickens.

MAKES 2 CUPS
Per tablespoon 14.4g fat; 589kJ

guacamole

2 medium avocados (500g)

1 medium white onion (150g), chopped finely

2 small tomatoes (260g), chopped finely

1 tablespoon lime juice

2 tablespoons coarsely chopped fresh coriander

Using a fork, mash avocado in medium bowl until almost smooth. Add onion, tomato, juice and coriander; mix well.

MAKES 3¼ CUPS
Per tablespoon 1.9g fat; 84kJ

24 crispy crab triangles

60g butter

3 green onions, chopped finely

1/4 cup (35g) plain flour

1 cup (250ml) milk

1 tablespoon lime juice

1 tablespoon finely chopped fresh flat-leaf parsley

2 x 170g cans crab meat, drained

16 sheets fillo pasty

180g butter, melted, extra

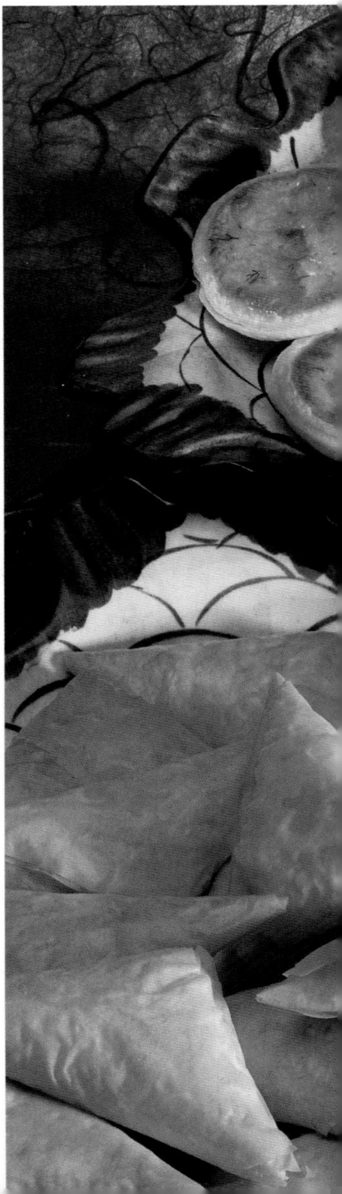

Melt butter in medium saucepan; cook onion, stirring, until soft. Add flour; cook, stirring, about 3 minutes or until mixture thickens and bubbles. Remove from heat, gradually stir in milk; cook, stirring, until mixture boils and thickens. Stir in juice, parsley and crab; cool to room temperature.
Preheat oven to moderate. Brush two sheets of the fillo with some of the extra butter, layer together; cut crossways into 7cm strips. Place a level teaspoon of crab mixture at bottom of one narrow edge of fillo strip. Fold opposite corner of fillo diagonally across the filling to form a triangle; continue folding to end of fillo strip, retaining triangular shape. Place triangles on lightly oiled oven trays, seam-side down; repeat with remaining pastry, extra butter and filling.
Brush triangles with remaining extra butter; bake, uncovered, in moderate oven about 15 minutes or until browned lightly.

MAKES 60
Per serving 3.6g fat; 197kJ

smoked salmon tartlets

3 sheets ready-rolled puff pastry

100g smoked salmon slices, chopped finely

2 gherkins, chopped finely

2 green onions, chopped finely

½ cup (120g) sour cream

1 tablespoon milk

2 eggs, beaten lightly

1 teaspoon finely chopped fresh dill

¼ teaspoon sweet paprika

Preheat oven to moderate. Cut 6.5cm rounds from pastry sheets (you need 24 rounds). Place rounds into lightly oiled 12-hole tart trays.
Sprinkle salmon, gherkin and onion into pastry shells; pour in combined cream, milk, egg, dill and paprika.
Bake, uncovered, in moderate oven about 30 minutes or until puffed and browned well.

MAKES 24
Per serving 7.4g fat; 465kJ

Top to bottom: smoked salmon tartlets; crispy crab triangles.

26 curried **beef** samosas

1 tablespoon vegetable oil

1 small brown onion (80g), chopped finely

1 clove garlic, crushed

1 teaspoon cumin seeds

1 tablespoon mild curry paste

150g minced beef

1 tablespoon finely chopped fresh coriander

1 small potato (120g), chopped finely

1/3 cup (80ml) water

125g spinach, chopped coarsely

8 x 25cm-square spring roll wrappers

1 egg, beaten lightly

vegetable oil, for deep-frying

Heat oil in small saucepan; cook onion, garlic, seeds and paste, stirring, until onion is soft. Add beef; cook, stirring, until browned. Stir in coriander, potato and the water; simmer, uncovered, until potato is tender. Stir in spinach; cook, uncovered, until most of the liquid has evaporated, cool.

Cut wrappers in half to form two rectangles. Brush one long side of each rectangle with egg. Spoon a tablespoon of beef mixture at bottom of one narrow edge of pastry rectangle. Fold opposite corner of pastry diagonally across the filling to form a triangle; continue folding to end of pastry sheet, retaining triangular shape. Repeat with remaining filling, wrappers and egg.

Heat oil in large saucepan; deep-fry samosas, in batches, until browned, drain on absorbent paper. Serve with mango chutney, if desired.

MAKES 16

Per serving 5.3g fat; 319kJ

chinese roast chicken wings

12 large chicken wings (1.5kg)

1/4 cup (60ml) light soy sauce

2 cloves garlic, crushed

1 teaspoon grated fresh ginger

2 tablespoons dry sherry

2 tablespoons honey

Cut wing tips from chicken at joint; reserve wing tips for another use. Place wings in large bowl with combined remaining ingredients. Cover; refrigerate 3 hours or overnight.

Preheat oven to moderate. Drain wings, reserve marinade. Place wings on oiled oven rack over baking dish. Bake, uncovered, in moderate oven, brushing occasionally with reserved marinade, about 45 minutes or until browned and cooked through.

MAKES 12

Per serving 7.2g fat; 580kJ

28 antipasto platter

300g kalamata olives

100g thinly sliced lamb prosciutto

100g thinly sliced spicy salami

pickled octopus

2kg baby octopus

1 cup (250ml) water

1 clove garlic, crushed

1 medium brown onion (150g), chopped finely

1 cup (250ml) white vinegar

½ cup (125ml) olive oil

roasted capsicums

4 medium yellow capsicums (800g)

4 medium red capsicums (800g)

½ cup (125ml) olive oil

3 cloves garlic, sliced thinly

2 tablespoons finely chopped fresh flat-leaf parsley

pesto salad

1½ cups tightly packed fresh basil

1 tablespoon pine nuts, toasted

1 clove garlic, crushed

2 tablespoons finely grated parmesan cheese

2 tablespoons olive oil

500g bocconcini cheese, chopped coarsely

250g cherry tomatoes, halved

Just before serving, arrange olives, prosciutto, salami, pickled octopus, roasted capsicums and pesto salad on large platter.

Pickled Octopus Discard heads and beaks from octopus; cut octopus into quarters. Combine octopus with the water in large saucepan; simmer, covered, about 1 hour or until octopus is tender. Drain; cool. Combine octopus with remaining ingredients in medium bowl, cover; refrigerate 3 hours or overnight.

Roasted Capsicums Quarter capsicums, remove and discard seeds and membranes. Roast under grill or in very hot oven, skin-side up, until skin blisters and blackens. Cover capsicum pieces with plastic or paper for 5 minutes, peel away skin, cut capsicum into thick strips. Toss capsicum with remaining ingredients in medium bowl.

Pesto Salad Blend or process basil, nuts, garlic, parmesan and oil until almost smooth. Toss bocconcini and tomato with pesto in medium bowl.

SERVES 10

Per serving
42g fat; 2518kJ

30 baked **fetta**

250g piece fetta

1/4 cup (60ml) olive oil

1/4 teaspoon sweet paprika

1 tablespoon finely chopped fresh oregano

4 black olives (20g), seeded, sliced thinly

Preheat oven to moderately hot. Place fetta on a 30cm piece of foil, drizzle with oil; sprinkle with remaining ingredients. Gather foil around fetta; fold over to seal.

Place on oven tray; bake in moderately hot oven about 20 minutes or until fetta is soft.

Serve warm with crusty bread, if desired.

SERVES 6

Per serving 18 [illegible] 0kJ

crunchy pork noodle balls 31

1 bundle (60g) dried egg noodles

250g minced pork

1 small red onion (100g), chopped finely

2 cloves garlic, crushed

2 teaspoons grated fresh ginger

1/3 cup coarsely chopped fresh coriander

1 egg yolk

1/4 cup (35g) plain flour

1 teaspoon sambal oelek

1 teaspoon fish sauce

peanut oil, for deep-frying

1/3 cup (80ml) sweet chilli sauce

2 tablespoons lime juice

Crumble noodles in a large heatproof bowl, cover with boiling water, stand 5 minutes or until tender; drain.
Combine noodles with pork, onion, garlic, ginger, coriander, egg yolk, flour, sambal and fish sauce in large bowl. Roll teaspoons of mixture into balls.
Heat oil in large saucepan; deep-fry pork balls, in batches, until browned and cooked through, drain on absorbent paper. Serve with combined sweet chilli sauce and juice.

MAK

Per 2g fat; 718kJ

32 four easy **dippers**

What's a party without dip? And what's a dip without dippers? These crunchy morsels are tasty with or without any of a wide selection of suitable accompaniments.

crisp turkish fingers

40cm loaf turkish pide

olive-oil spray

Cut pide into 2cm-wide strips, place in single layer on oven tray. Coat with olive-oil spray; grill until browned lightly.

MAKES 20
Per serving 0.8g fat; 255kJ

spicy pitta crisps

4 large pittas

olive-oil spray

1/2 teaspoon cajun seasoning

Preheat oven to moderately hot. Split pitta in half; cut each half into eight wedges. Place wedges, split-side up, in single layer on oven trays, coat with olive-oil spray; sprinkle with seasoning. **Bake**, uncovered, in moderately hot oven about 5 minutes or until crisp.

MAKES 64
Per serving 0.2g fat; 58kJ

pesto pizza wedges

25cm prepared pizza base

1 tablespoon basil pesto

½ cup (50g) grated pizza cheese

2 teaspoons olive oil

Preheat oven to moderately hot. Place pizza base on lightly oiled pizza tray, spread with pesto; sprinkle with cheese. Drizzle pizza with oil.
Bake, uncovered, in moderately hot oven about 15 minutes or until browned and crisp. Cut into 16 wedges to serve.

MAKES 16
Per serving 2.3g fat; 253kJ

cheesy pastry twists

1 sheet ready-rolled puff pastry, thawed

1 egg, beaten lightly

2 tablespoons finely grated cheddar cheese

2 tablespoons finely grated parmesan cheese

Preheat oven to hot. Brush one side of pastry sheet with egg, then sprinkle with combined cheeses. Cut pastry sheet in half; cut each half, widthways, into 1cm strips. Twist pastry pieces; place on lightly oiled oven trays.
Bake, uncovered, in hot oven about 10 minutes or until pastry is browned and puffed. Transfer to wire racks to cool.

MAKES 50
Per serving 1.1g fat; 69kJ

34 prawn and crab wontons

500g large uncooked prawns

500g crabmeat

1 teaspoon grated fresh ginger

1 clove garlic, crushed

4 green onions, chopped finely

1 tablespoon light soy sauce

1 tablespoon sweet chilli sauce

80 wonton wrappers

1 tablespoon cornflour

1 tablespoon water

peanut oil, for deep-frying

dipping sauce

2 teaspoons light soy sauce

2 tablespoons sweet chilli sauce

1 teaspoon dry sherry

1 green onion, chopped finely

Shell and devein prawns; chop prawn meat finely.

Combine prawn meat in medium bowl with crab, ginger, garlic, onion and sauces. Place a heaped teaspoon of prawn mixture in centre of each wrapper; brush edges with blended cornflour and water, pinch edges together to seal.

Heat oil in large saucepan; deep-fry wontons, in batches, until browned and cooked through. Drain on absorbent paper; serve with dipping sauce.

Dipping Sauce Combine ingredients in small bowl.

MAKES 80

Per serving
1.1g fat; 105kJ

bombay-spiced chicken skewers

1 cup (250ml) peanut oil

4 cloves garlic, crushed

2 tablespoons sweet paprika

1 tablespoon ground cumin

1 tablespoon ground turmeric

1 tablespoon ground coriander

2kg chicken breast fillets

raita

2 lebanese cucumbers (260g), seeded, chopped finely

3/4 cup (200g) yogurt

1 tablespoon lemon juice

2 cloves garlic, crushed

1/4 cup finely chopped fresh mint

Heat oil in small saucepan; cook garlic and spices, stirring, until fragrant.

Cut chicken into 3cm pieces; thread onto 24 skewers. Place skewers in large shallow dish or oven tray, pour over spiced oil mixture; turn skewers to coat well. Cover; refrigerate 3 hours or overnight.

Drain skewers; discard oil mixture. Cook skewers, in batches, on heated oiled grill plate (or grill or barbecue) until browned all over and cooked through. Serve with raita.

Raita Combine ingredients in small bowl.

MAKES 24

Per serving
14.7g fat; 1614kJ

36 mini pizza swirls

1 teaspoon sugar

2 teaspoons (7g) dried yeast

1/4 cup (60ml) warm water

1 1/2 cups (225g) plain flour

1 teaspoon salt

1 tablespoon vegetable oil

1/2 cup (125ml) warm water, approximately, extra

tomato sauce

1 teaspoon olive oil

1 clove garlic, crushed

1/2 cup (140g) tomato paste

2 tablespoons tomato sauce

1 teaspoon dried oregano

topping

4 green onions, chopped finely

1/2 small green capsicum (75g), chopped finely

2 hard-boiled eggs, chopped coarsely

1/3 cup (35g) coarsely grated mozzarella cheese

Combine sugar, yeast and the water in small bowl, cover; stand in warm place about 10 minutes or until frothy.

Sift flour and salt into large bowl, stir in yeast mixture, oil and enough extra water to mix to a soft dough. Knead dough on floured surface about 10 minutes or until smooth.

Place dough in large oiled bowl, cover; stand in warm place about 45 minutes or until doubled in size.

Preheat oven to moderate. Knead dough on floured surface until smooth. Roll half of the dough into a 20cm x 45cm rectangle; spread with half of the tomato sauce, sprinkle with half of the topping. Roll up tightly from the long side; cut into 1cm slices. Place slices, cut-side up, on lightly oiled oven trays. Repeat with remaining dough, tomato sauce and topping. Bake, uncovered, in moderate oven about 15 minutes or until browned.

Tomato Sauce Heat oil in small frying pan; cook garlic, stirring, until fragrant. Stir in paste, sauce and oregano; cool.

Topping Combine ingredients in small bowl.

MAKES 60

Per serving 0.8g fat; 101kJ

38 spiced lentil and hummus toasts

28cm bread stick

2 teaspoons olive oil

1 small brown onion (80g), finely chopped

1 clove garlic, crushed

1 teaspoon ground cumin

1 teaspoon ground coriander

1/2 teaspoon sweet paprika

1/2 cup (100g) red lentils, rinsed, drained

1/2 x 400g can tomatoes

3/4 cup (180ml) vegetable stock

2 tablespoons chopped fresh mint

2/3 cup (180g) hummus

Trim ends from bread, cut diagonally into 1cm slices. Grill slices until browned. **Heat** oil in pan, add onion and garlic; cook, stirring, until soft. Add spices; cook, stirring, until fragrant. Stir in lentils, undrained crushed tomatoes and stock. Simmer gently, covered, about 20 minutes, stirring occasionally, until lentils are tender and most of the liquid is absorbed; cool. Stir in half of the mint. **Divide** lentil mixture among toasts; top with teaspoons of hummus, then remaining mint.

MAKES 25

Per serving 2g fat; 200kJ

crunchy thai chicken rounds

250g minced chicken
2 tablespoons coconut milk
1½ tablespoons sweet chilli sauce
2 teaspoons finely chopped fresh lemon grass
1½ tablespoons lemon juice
2 tablespoons finely chopped fresh coriander
1 clove garlic, crushed
2 large green cucumbers (800g)

Cook chicken in heated medium non-stick frying pan, stirring, until browned lightly; cool 5 minutes. Process chicken until finely chopped.
Combine chicken with coconut milk, sauce, lemon grass, juice, coriander and garlic in medium bowl, cover; refrigerate 3 hours or overnight.
Cut cucumbers diagonally into 1cm slices. Divide chicken mixture among slices, top with coriander leaves, if desired.

MAKES 25
Per serving 1.2g fat; 98kJ

40 tuna nori rolls

2 cups (400g) koshihikari rice

1/3 cup (80ml) rice vinegar

2 tablespoons sugar

1/4 teaspoon salt

6 sheets toasted nori

120g sashimi tuna, sliced thinly

1 lebanese cucumber (130g), seeded, sliced thinly

1 small avocado (200g), sliced thinly

2 tablespoons pickled ginger slices

1/2 teaspoon wasabi

Add rice to large saucepan of boiling water; boil, uncovered, until just tender. Drain, stand rice 5 minutes; stir in vinegar, sugar and salt, cool.

Place one sheet of nori, rough-side up, on bamboo sushi mat. Dip fingers in water and spread one-sixth of the rice mixture over nori, leaving a 4cm strip on short side closest to you; press rice firmly in place. Using fingers, make a lengthways hollow across centre of rice. Place one-sixth of each of the tuna, cucumber, avocado, ginger and wasabi in hollow centre of rice.

Starting at edge closest to you, use mat to help roll the tuna nori, pressing firmly as you roll. Remove mat from finished nori roll. Cut roll into six pieces and place on serving plate; repeat with remaining ingredients.

Serve tuna nori rolls with soy sauce, extra pickled ginger and extra wasabi, if desired.

MAKES 36 PIECES

Per serving 1.1g fat; 242kJ

42 moroccan-style lamb cutlets

24 french-trimmed lamb cutlets (1.5kg)

1/4 cup (40g) moroccan seasoning

250g prepared baba ghanoush

2 teaspoons cumin seeds, toasted

green onion stems, for garnish, optional

Lightly coat lamb with seasoning. Char-grill (or grill or barbecue) lamb cutlets until browned both sides and cooked as desired.
Top each lamb cutlet with a teaspoon of baba ghanoush and a few cumin seeds.
If using the green onion stems for garnish, dip briefly into boiling water, then tie on the ends of cutlet bones; trim ends of onions.

MAKES 24
Per serving 5.2g fat; 352kJ

cheese and semi-dried tomato puffs

1 sheet ready-rolled butter puff pastry

100g boursin cheese

1/4 cup (65g) bottled sun-dried tomato pesto

25 (100g) drained semi-dried tomatoes in oil

25 small fresh basil leaves

Preheat oven to moderate. Cut 5cm squares from pastry sheet (you need 25 squares). Place the pastry squares on lightly oiled oven tray; prick each square all over with a fork.
Bake, uncovered, in moderate oven about 20 minutes or until pastry is browned.
Just before serving, spread pastry squares with cheese; top with a little pesto, then the tomatoes and basil leaves.

MAKES 25
Per serving 3.2g fat; 203kJ

44 baba ghanoush

2 large eggplants (1kg)

¼ cup (70g) yogurt

2 tablespoons lemon juice

1 clove garlic, crushed

¼ cup (60ml) tahini

2 teaspoons ground cumin

⅓ cup loosely packed fresh coriander leaves

Preheat oven to hot. Pierce eggplants in several places with a skewer. Place whole eggplants on oven tray. Bake, uncovered, in hot oven about 1 hour or until soft; cool 15 minutes.

Peel eggplants, chop flesh coarsely; discard skins. Blend or process eggplant flesh with remaining ingredients until combined. Sprinkle with chopped parsley and serve with pitta, if desired.

MAKES 2¼ CUPS

Per tablespoon

1.6g fat; 101kJ

nachos bites

230g packet plain corn chips

1 cup (270g) canned refried beans

1/4 cup (60g) sour cream

1 tablespoon finely chopped fresh coriander

2 teaspoons cajun seasoning

1 cup (125g) finely grated cheddar cheese

2 small tomatoes (260g), seeded, sliced thinly

1 small avocado (200g), chopped finely

2 tablespoons finely chopped fresh flat-leaf parsley

Preheat oven to moderately hot. Select 60 large, unbroken chips, place in single layer on lightly oiled oven trays. Top chips with combined beans, cream, coriander and seasoning; sprinkle with cheese.
Just before serving, bake, uncovered, in moderately hot oven about 8 minutes or until cheese is melted and chips are crisp.
Cut tomato slices into small pieces; top each chip with tomato and avocado, sprinkle with parsley.

MAKES 60
Per serving 2.8g fat; 168kJ

46 creamy chicken and almond ribbon sandwiches

850g chicken breast fillets

4 sticks trimmed celery (300g), sliced thinly

24 slices white sandwich bread

1/2 cup (40g) flaked almonds, toasted

mayonnaise

2 egg yolks

1 tablespoon lemon juice

2 teaspoons dijon mustard

1 cup (250ml) olive oil

Add chicken to large shallow pan of simmering water; simmer gently, uncovered, 15 minutes or until just cooked through. Remove from pan; cool. Chop chicken finely, then place in a large bowl with mayonnaise and celery; mix well.

Divide chicken mixture among 12 bread slices; sprinkle with almonds; top with remaining bread slices. Using an electric or serrated knife, remove and discard crusts from bread; cut each sandwich into three fingers.

Mayonnaise Blend or process egg yolks, juice and mustard until smooth. With motor operating, add oil gradually in thin stream; process until mixture thickens.

MAKES 36

Per serving 9g fat; 578kJ

pesto pastry stars

30g butter, softened

2 tablespoons basil pesto

2 sheets ready-rolled butter puff pastry

1/2 cup (40g) finely grated parmesan cheese

Preheat oven to moderately hot. Combine butter and pesto in small bowl. Spread pesto mixture over pastry sheets; sprinkle with cheese. **Using** a 5.5cm cutter, cut stars from pastry sheets; place onto lightly oiled oven trays. Bake, uncovered, in moderately hot oven about 10 minutes or until puffed and browned; cool.

MAKES 40

Per serving 3.2g fat; 187kJ

48 tahini dip

12 cloves garlic

2 teaspoons ground cumin

1 teaspoon finely grated lemon rind

2/3 cup (160ml) tahini

1/2 cup (125ml) lemon juice

1/2 cup (125ml) water

Preheat oven to hot. Place unpeeled garlic cloves on oven tray; bake, uncovered, in hot oven about 10 minutes or until garlic is soft, cool. Remove skin from cloves.

Blend or process garlic, cumin, rind and tahini until combined. With motor operating, gradually add combined juice and water in thin stream; process until combined. Spoon into serving bowl; sprinkle with a little extra ground cumin and serve with toasted pitta, if desired.

MAKES 1 1/2 CUPS

Per tablespoon 5.5g fat; 250kJ

homemade sausage **rolls** 49

2 large potatoes (600g), quartered

2 teaspoons vegetable oil

1 large brown onion (200g), grated coarsely

2 cloves garlic, crushed

1 teaspoon ground cumin

1 teaspoon mild curry powder

300g sausage mince

200g minced beef

4 sheets ready-rolled puff pastry

1 egg, beaten lightly

Boil, steam or microwave potato until just tender; drain, mash in medium bowl.

Heat oil in small frying pan; cook onion, garlic and spices, stirring, until onion is soft and liquid has evaporated. Combine onion mixture in large bowl with potato and minces; mix well.

Preheat oven to hot. Cut each pastry sheet in half; divide the mince mixture among pastry halves. Shape mince mixture down one long side of pastry; brush around edges with egg, roll to enclose filling. Cut rolls in half; brush with egg, score top of each roll with sharp knife. Place rolls, seam-side down, on lightly oiled oven trays. Bake, uncovered, in hot oven about 25 minutes or until browned.

MAKES 16

Per serving 16g fat; 1101kJ

50 vietnamese

spring rolls

1 medium red capsicum (200g) Pepper

1 medium carrot (120g)

1 tablespoon peanut oil

700g chicken breast fillets

100g bean thread noodles

1 tablespoon grated fresh ginger

2 cloves garlic, crushed

4 green onions, chopped finely

1 tablespoon finely chopped fresh vietnamese mint

500g bok choy, shredded finely

1/4 cup (60ml) sweet chilli sauce

1 tablespoon light soy sauce

40 x 25cm-square spring roll wrappers

vegetable oil, for deep-frying

dipping sauce

1/3 cup (80ml) sweet chilli sauce

2 tablespoons lime juice

3 green onions, chopped finely

Halve capsicum; remove and discard seeds and membranes. Slice capsicum and carrot into paper-thin strips.

Heat half of the oil in medium saucepan; cook chicken, in batches, until browned and cooked through. Cool 10 minutes; shred finely.

Meanwhile, place noodles in large heatproof bowl; cover with boiling water, stand 2 minutes. Drain noodles; chop coarsely. Heat remaining oil in same pan; cook ginger, garlic and onion, stirring, about 2 minutes or until onion is soft.

Combine carrot, capsicum, chicken, noodles and onion mixture in large bowl with mint, bok choy and sauces. Place a rounded tablespoon of mixture across edge of one wrapper; roll to enclose filling, folding in ends. Place on tray, seam-side down. Repeat with remaining mixture and wrappers, placing on tray in single layer.

Just before serving, heat oil in large saucepan; deep-fry spring rolls, in batches, until golden brown and cooked through. Drain on absorbent paper; serve with dipping sauce.

Dipping Sauce Combine ingredients in small bowl.

MAKES 40

Per serving 4.3g fat; 307kJ

52 pesto dip with crisp garlic wedges

1 cup coarsely chopped fresh basil

1 clove garlic, crushed

2 tablespoons pine nuts, toasted

2 tablespoons finely grated parmesan cheese

2 tablespoons olive oil

2 teaspoons lemon juice

1¼ cups (300g) sour cream

crisp garlic wedges

4 large pittas

150g butter, melted

2 cloves garlic, crushed

⅔ cup (50g) finely grated parmesan cheese

Blend or process basil, garlic, nuts, cheese, oil and juice until smooth. Combine in medium bowl with cream; serve with crisp garlic wedges. **Crisp Garlic Wedges** Preheat oven to moderately hot. Split pitta in half, cut each half into eight wedges; place, split-side up, on oven trays. Brush with combined butter and garlic, sprinkle with cheese. Bake, uncovered, in moderately hot oven about 8 minutes or until browned lightly and crisp.

MAKES 1½ CUPS DIP AND 64 WEDGES
Per tablespoon of dip 10g fat; 398kJ
Per wedge 2.3g fat; 142kJ

cajun potato **wedges**

8 medium potatoes (1.6kg)

1/4 cup (60ml) olive oil

90g butter, melted

2 tablespoons ground cumin

2 tablespoons cajun seasoning

pesto dipping sauce

1 1/4 cups (300g) sour cream

1/4 cup (65g) bottled basil pesto

1/4 cup (20g) finely grated parmesan cheese

sweet chilli dipping sauce

1/3 cup (80ml) sweet chilli sauce

1 1/4 cups (300g) sour cream

Cut unpeeled potatoes in half, cut each half into four wedges. Boil, steam or microwave potatoes until just tender; drain, cool. Preheat oven to hot.
Combine oil, butter and spices in large bowl, add wedges, in batches; coat evenly with spice mixture. Place wedges on oven trays. Bake, uncovered, in hot oven about 45 minutes or until crisp. Serve with Dipping Sauces.
Pesto Dipping Sauce Combine ingredients in medium bowl.
Sweet Chilli Dipping Sauce Combine ingredients in medium bowl.

MAKES 2 CUPS EACH SAUCE AND 64 WEDGES
Per wedge 2.1g fat; 148kJ
Per tablespoon pesto dip 6.3g fat; 255kJ
Per tablespoon chilli dip 5.1g fat; 211kJ

avocado pistachio pâté with herb toasts

You will need about two medium avocados (500g) for this recipe.

1½ cups mashed avocado

125g packaged cream cheese

2 green onions, chopped finely

1 clove garlic, crushed

1 teaspoon lemon juice

¼ teaspoon chilli powder

2 tablespoons finely chopped pistachios

1 teaspoon finely chopped fresh flat-leaf parsley

herb toasts

2 large pitta

40g butter, melted

½ teaspoon dried rosemary

½ teaspoon dried basil

½ teaspoon dried thyme

Blend or process avocado, cheese, onion, garlic, juice and chilli until smooth.

Line two 1-cup (250ml) moulds with plastic wrap, sprinkle nuts into base of each mould; pour in avocado mixture. Cover; refrigerate about 3 hours or until set. Turn out of moulds, sprinkle with parsley; serve with herb toasts.

Herb Toasts Preheat oven to moderate. Split pitta in half, brush spilt side with butter; sprinkle with combined herbs. Place pitta, split-side up, on oven trays; bake, uncovered, in moderate oven about 10 minutes or until browned lightly and crisp, cool. Break each piece of pitta into six pieces.

MAKES 2 CUPS DIP AND 24 HERB TOASTS

Per tablespoon pâté
5.7g fat; 233kJ

per toast 1.5g fat; 126kJ

56 caramelised **onion** and goat cheese tarts

20g butter

2 large brown onions (400g), sliced thinly

1 clove garlic, crushed

1 tablespoon brown sugar

2 teaspoons balsamic vinegar

1 tablespoon water

1 sheet ready-rolled butter puff pastry

30g goat cheese (or fetta), crumbled

1 tablespoon fresh thyme sprigs

Melt butter in medium frying pan; cook onion and garlic, stirring, over low heat about 30 minutes or until onion is very soft and browned. Add sugar, vinegar and the water; cook, stirring, until onion is caramelised.

Meanwhile, preheat oven to hot. Cut 3.5cm rounds from pastry sheet (you need 36 rounds). Place pastry rounds on oiled oven tray. Bake, uncovered, in hot oven about 15 minutes or until browned and puffed; cool.

Just before serving, top pastry rounds with warm onion mixture, cheese and thyme.

MAKES 36

Per serving 1.7g fat; 117kJ

red-curry crab cakes with chilli-lime dipping sauce

2 x 170g cans crab meat, drained

650g large uncooked prawns, shelled, deveined

1 tablespoon thai-style red curry paste

1 egg

2 green onions, chopped coarsely

2 tablespoons finely chopped fresh coriander

2 teaspoons finely chopped fresh lemon grass

1 red thai chilli, seeded, quartered

2 tablespoons peanut oil

chilli-lime dipping sauce

2 tablespoons lime juice

2 tablespoons water

2 teaspoons fish sauce

2 teaspoons sugar

1 fresh kaffir lime leaf, shredded finely

1 red thai chilli, seeded, chopped finely

Process crab, prawns, paste, egg, onion, coriander, lemon grass and chilli until just combined. Shape level tablespoons of mixture into patties.

Heat oil in large frying pan; cook crab cakes, in batches, until browned both sides and cooked through, drain. Serve hot crab cakes with chilli-lime dipping sauce.

Chilli-Lime Dipping Sauce Combine ingredients in small bowl, stirring, until sugar dissolves.

MAKES 30

Per serving 1.7g fat; 133kJ

58 smoked salmon and caper pizzas

2 sheets ready-rolled butter puff pastry

1 cup (200g) ricotta cheese

3 teaspoons hot water

2 tablespoons finely chopped fresh chives

3 teaspoons horseradish cream

6 slices (180g) smoked salmon, chopped coarsely

2 tablespoons drained capers

6 sprigs fresh dill

Preheat oven to very hot. Cut 5.5cm rounds from pastry sheets (you need 16 rounds). Place on lightly oiled oven trays. Bake, uncovered, in very hot oven about 8 minutes or until browned, cool. Split rounds in half. **Combine** ricotta and the water in medium bowl; stir in chives and cream. Just before serving, spread ricotta mixture over rounds; top with salmon, capers and dill sprigs.

MAKES 32

r serving 3.4g fat; 237kJ

marinated grilled prawns

20 large uncooked prawns (1kg)

1 medium brown onion (150g), chopped coarsely

1/2 cup (140g) yogurt

1/2 teaspoon ground turmeric

1/2 teaspoon chilli powder

1 tablespoon sweet paprika

1 teaspoon grated fresh ginger

2 cloves garlic, quartered

1 tablespoon lemon juice

Wash prawns; pat dry with absorbent paper. Remove heads and legs, leaving tails and body shells intact.
Blend or process remaining ingredients until smooth. Combine yogurt mixture and prawns in large bowl, cover; refrigerate overnight.
Grill or barbecue prawns until tender, brushing occasionally with marinade during cooking.

MAKES 20
Per serving 0.5g fat; 128kJ

glossary

baba ghanoush commercially prepared eggplant dip; available in supermarkets.

bacon rashers also known as slices of bacon; made from cured, smoked pork.

bean thread noodles also known as cellophane or glass noodles; made from green mung bean flour.

beetroot also known as red beets or simply beets; firm, round root vegetable.

bocconcini cheese rounds of fresh "baby" mozzarella sold in brine; semi-soft white cheese.

bok choy also called pak choi or Chinese white cabbage; has a mild mustard taste.

boursin cheese soft, cow-milk cream cheese flavoured with garlic and herbs.

breadcrumbs, stale one- or two-day-old bread made into crumbs by grating, blending or processing.

butter use salted or unsalted ("sweet") butter; 125g is equal to one stick of butter.

cajun seasoning packaged blend of assorted herbs and spices, including basil, paprika, tarragon, cayenne, onion, fennel and thyme.

capsicum also known as bell pepper or, simply, pepper. Discard seeds and membranes before use.

chilli, thai small chilli that is medium-hot and dark-green to bright-red in colour.

chilli jam commercially prepared jam; available from some supermarkets and delicatessens. Substitute tomato chilli relish or chutney.

cornflour also known as cornstarch; used as a thickening agent.

corn relish a thick spread consisting of corn, celery, onion, capsicum, spices and mustard. Available from supermarkets.

cream

cheese: soft, milk cheese; available commercially as "Philadelphia" or "Philly".

sour: (minimum fat content 35%) thick, commercially-cultured soured cream.

eggs some recipes use raw or barely-cooked eggs; show caution if salmonella is a problem in your area.

fetta cheese crumbly-textured goat- or sheep-milk cheese with a sharp, salty taste.

fish sauce also known as nam pla or nuoc nam; made from pulverised, salted, fermented fish. Has a pungent smell and strong taste; use sparingly.

five-spice powder fragrant blend of ground cinnamon, cloves, star anise, sichuan pepper and fennel seeds.

flour, plain all-purpose flour, made from wheat.

gherkin also known as a cornichon; young, dark-green pickled cucumbers.

hoisin sauce a thick, sweet and spicy paste made from salted fermented soy beans, onions and garlic.

horseradish cream creamy prepared paste of grated horseradish, vinegar, oil and sugar.

hummus commercially prepared chickpea dip; available in supermarkets.

kaffir lime leaves fresh aromatic leaves of a small citrus tree; available from many Asian food stores.

koshihikari rice small, round-grain white rice. Substitute white short-grain rice; cook by the absorption method.

kumara orange-fleshed sweet potato often confused with yam.

lemon grass a tall, clumping, lemon-smelling and -tasting, sharp-edged grass; use white, lower part of stem.

mince also known as ground meat (beef, pork, chicken, pork and veal).

moroccan seasoning prepared blends include black pepper, cinnamon, cloves, coriander, cumin, nutmeg, paprika, rosemary and turmeric.

nori, toasted dried seaweed sold in paper-thin sheets.

oil

peanut: pressed from ground peanuts; ideal for stir-fry cooking because of its high smoke point.

sesame: made from roasted, crushed white sesame seeds. Used for flavour, rather than as a cooking medium.

onion

green: also known as scallion or (incorrectly) shallot; an immature onion picked before the bulb has formed, having a long, bright-green edible stalk.

red: also known as Spanish, red Spanish or Bermuda onion; a sweet-flavoured, large, purple-red onion.

pitta large, flat rounds of wheat-flour Lebanese bread.

prawns crustacean also known as shrimp.

prosciutto salted-cured, air-dried (unsmoked), pressed ham-like meat; usually sold in paper-thin slices, ready to eat, and made from pork, lamb or beef.

refried beans pinto beans cooked twice: soaked and boiled, then mashed and fried, traditionally in lard. Available in cans from supermarkets.

rice vinegar also known as seasoned rice vinegar. Made from fermented rice; colourless, flavoured with sugar and salt.

ricotta cheese sweet, moist, fresh curd cheese having a low fat content.

sambal oelek (also ulek or olek) Indonesian in origin; a salty paste made from ground chillies and vinegar.

silverbeet also known as Swiss chard and, incorrectly, spinach; a member of the beet family grown for its tasty green leaves and celery-like stems.

spinach leafy vegetable; often called english spinach or, incorrectly, silverbeet. A small, or "baby", variety can be eaten raw in salads.

tahini a rich, buttery paste made from crushed sesame seeds; used in making hummus and other Middle-Eastern sauces.

tarama salted, dried roe of the grey mullet fish.

tuna, sashimi freshest and best-quality yellowfin or bluefin tuna, sold as suitable for eating raw.

vietnamese mint narrow-leafed pungent herb, also known as cambodian mint, daun laksa and laksa leaf.

wasabi an Asian horseradish used to make a fiery sauce traditionally served with Japanese food; sold as paste, in a tube, or powdered in cans.

yeast a 7g (¼oz) sachet of dried yeast (2 teaspoons) is equal to 15g (½oz) compressed yeast if using one in place of the other.

index

facts and figures 63

These conversions are approximate only, but the difference between an exact and the approximate conversion of various liquid and dry measures is minimal and will not affect your cooking results.

Measuring equipment

The difference between one country's measuring cups and another's is, at most, within a 2 or 3 teaspoon variance. (For the record, 1 Australian metric measuring cup holds approximately 250ml.) The most accurate way of measuring dry ingredients is to weigh them. For liquids, use a clear glass or plastic jug having metric markings.

Note: NZ, Canada, USA and UK all use 15ml tablespoons. Australian tablespoons measure 20ml.
All cup and spoon measurements are level.

How to measure

When using graduated measuring cups, shake dry ingredients loosely into the appropriate cup. Do not tap the cup on a bench or tightly pack the ingredients unless directed to do so. Level the top of measuring cups and measuring spoons with a knife. When measuring liquids, place a clear glass or plastic jug having metric markings on a flat surface to check accuracy at eye level.

Dry Measures

metric	imperial
15g	1/2oz
30g	1oz
60g	2oz
90g	3oz
125g	4oz (1/4lb)
155g	5oz
185g	6oz
220g	7oz
250g	8oz (1/2lb)
280g	9oz
315g	10oz
345g	11oz
375g	12oz (3/4lb)
410g	13oz
440g	14oz
470g	15oz
500g	16oz (1lb)
750g	24oz (1 1/2lb)
1kg	32oz (2lb)

We use large eggs having an average weight of 60g.

Liquid Measures

metric	imperial
30ml	1 fluid oz
60ml	2 fluid oz
100ml	3 fluid oz
125ml	4 fluid oz
150ml	5 fluid oz (1/4 pint/1 gill)
190ml	6 fluid oz
250ml (1cup)	8 fluid oz
300ml	10 fluid oz (1/2 pint)
500ml	16 fluid oz
600ml	20 fluid oz (1 pint)
1000ml (1litre)	1 3/4 pints

Helpful Measures

metric	imperial
3mm	1/8in
6mm	1/4in
1cm	1/2in
2cm	3/4in
2.5cm	1in
6cm	2 1/2in
8cm	3in
20cm	8in
23cm	9in
25cm	10in
30cm	12in (1ft)

Oven Temperatures

These oven temperatures are only a guide.
Always check the manufacturer's manual.

	°C (Celsius)	°F (Fahrenheit)	Gas Mark
Very slow	120	250	1
Slow	150	300	2
Moderately slow	160	325	3
Moderate	180 – 190	350 – 375	4
Moderately hot	200 – 210	400 – 425	5
Hot	220 – 230	450 – 475	6
Very hot	240 – 250	500 – 525	7

at your fingertips

These elegant slipcovers store up to 10 mini books and make the books instantly accessible.

And the metric measuring cups and spoons make following our recipes a piece of cake.

Book Holder
Australia and overseas: $A8.95 (incl. GST).

Metric Measuring Set
Australia: $6.50 (incl. GST).
New Zealand: $A8.00.
Elsewhere: $A9.95.
Prices include postage and handling.
This offer is available in all countries.

Mail or fax Photocopy and complete the coupon below and post to AWW Home Library Reader Offer, ACP Direct, PO Box 7036, Sydney NSW 1028, *or* fax to (02) 9267 4363.

Phone Have your credit card details ready, then, if you live in Sydney, phone 9260 0000; if you live elsewhere in Australia, phone 1800 252 515 (free call, Mon-Fri, 8.30am - 5.30pm).

Australian residents We accept the credit cards listed on the coupon, money orders and cheques.

Overseas residents We accept the credit cards listed on the coupon, drafts in $A drawn on an Australian bank, and also British, New Zealand and U.S. cheques in the currency of the country of issue.

Photocopy and complete the coupon below

☐ **Book holder** ☐ **Metric measuring set**

Please indicate number(s) required.

Mr/Mrs/Ms ______________________

Address ______________________

____

Postcode ______________ Country ______________

Phone: Business hours (   ) ______________

I enclose my cheque/money order for $________ payable to ACP Direct

OR: please charge $ ________ to my: ☐ Bankcard ☐ Visa

☐ Amex ☐ MasterCard ☐ Diners Club Expiry Date ___/___

☐☐☐☐☐☐☐☐☐☐☐☐☐☐☐☐

C... ...lder's signature ______________________

...low up to 30 days for delivery within Australia.

... 6 weeks for overseas deliveries. Both offers expire 31/12/02.

Food editor Pamela Clark
Associate food editor Karen Hammial
Assistant food editor Kathy McGarry
Assistant recipe editor Elizabeth Hooper

HOME LIBRARY STAFF
Editor-in-chief Susan Tomnay
Editor Julie Collard
Concept design Jackie Richards
Designer Caryl Wiggins
Book sales manager Jennifer McDonald
Production manager Carol Currie

Publisher Sue Wannan
Group publisher Jill Baker
Chief executive officer John Alexander

Produced by *The Australian Women's Weekly* Home Library, Sydney.

Colour separations by ACP Colour Graphics Pty Ltd, Sydney.
Printing by Dai Nippon Printing in Hong Kong.

Published by ACP Publishing Pty Limited, 54 Park St, Sydney; GPO Box 4088, Sydney, NSW 1028. Ph: (02) 9282 8618 Fax: (02) 9267 9438.

awwhomelib@acp.com.au
www.awwbooks.com.au

Australia Distributed by Network Distribution Company, GPO Box 4088, Sydney, NSW 1028. Ph: (02) 9282 8777 Fax: (02) 9264 3278.

United Kingdom Distributed by Australian Consolidated Press (UK), Moulton Park Busines Centre, Red House Road, Moulton Park, Northampton, NN3 6AQ. Ph: (01604) 497 531 Fax: (01604) 497 533 acpukltd@aol.com

Canada Distributed by Whitecap Books Ltd, 351 Lynn Ave, North Vancouver, BC, V7J 2C4, Ph: (604) 980 9852.

New Zealand Distributed by Netlink Distribution Company, Level 4, 23 Hargreaves St, College Hill, Auckland 1, Ph: (9) 302 7616.

South Africa Distributed by: PSD Promotions (Pty) Ltd, PO Box 1175, Isando 1600, SA, Ph: (011) 392 6065; and CNA Limited, Newsstand Division, PO Box 1079 Johannesburg 2000. Ph: (011) 491 7500.

Bites.

Includes index.
ISBN 1 86396 243 3

1. Snack foods. 2. Appetizers.
I. Title: Australian Women's Weekly.
(Series: Australian Women's Weekly Creative Food mini series).

641.812

Cover: Smoked salmon and caper pizzas, page 58.
Stylist: Cherise Koch
Photographer: Ian Hofstetter
Back cover: Empanadas, page 8.

The publishers would like to thank Andersons, Moore Park, NSW, for props used in photograph